The Wampanoag
and Their History

by Natalie M. Rosinsky

Content Adviser: Bruce Bernstein, Ph.D.,
Assistant Director for Cultural Resources,
National Museum of the American Indian, Smithsonian Institution

Reading Adviser: Rosemary G. Palmer, Ph.D.,
Department of Literacy, College of Education,
Boise State University

COMPASS POINT BOOKS
MINNEAPOLIS, MINNESOTA

Compass Point Books
3109 West 50th Street, #115
Minneapolis, MN 55410

Visit Compass Point Books on the Internet at *www.compasspointbooks.com*
or e-mail your request to *custserv@compasspointbooks.com*

On the cover: A 1772 colored engraving of Metacom (King Philip) by Paul Revere

Photographs ©: The Granger Collection, New York, cover; Prints Old & Rare, back cover (far left); Library of Congress, back cover, 30; Hulton Archive/Getty Images, 4; MPI/Getty Images, 5, 32; Kean Collection/Getty Images, 7; Richard Berenholtz/Corbis, 8-9; Marilyn "Angel" Wynn, 11, 12, 13, 14, 15, 16, 17, 19, 20, 21, 22, 23, 27, 31, 37, 39, 40, 41; North Wind Picture Archives, 24, 25, 28, 33, 34; Lee Snider/Photo Images/Corbis, 36; AP Photo/Stew Milne, 38; John Cross/The Free Press, 48.

Creative Director: Terri Foley
Managing Editor: Catherine Neitge
Art Director: Keith Griffin
Photo Researcher: Marcie C. Spence
Designer/Page production: Bradfordesign, Inc./Les Tranby
Cartographer: XNR Productions, Inc.
Educational Consultant: Diane Smolinski

Library of Congress Cataloging-in-Publication Data
Rosinsky, Natalie M. (Natalie Myra)
  The Wampanoag and their history / by Natalie M. Rosinsky.
     p. cm. — (We the people)
  Includes bibliographical references and index.
  ISBN 0-7565-0847-9 (hardcover)
  1. Wampanoag Indians—History—Juvenile literature. 2. Wampanoag Indians—Social life and customs—Juvenile literature. I. Title. II. We the people (Series) (Compass Point Books)
  E99.W2R67 2005
  974.4004'97348—dc22   2004018967

TABLE OF CONTENTS

A SHOT RANG OUT!

A small group of colonists crept silently toward their sleeping enemy. They hoped to surprise him just before dawn on that hot summer day of August 12, 1686. The swampy land they crawled through was located in what is now Bristol, Rhode Island. These armed men were hunting Metacom, the Wampanoag chief who they called King Philip. For more than a year, he had led local Indian tribes in deadly attacks on English colonists. This conflict came to be known as King Philip's War.

Chief Metacom was known as King Philip

A musket shot rang out! Philip jumped up but could not outrun his enemies. He was shot through the heart. Captain Benjamin Church, who led the colonists that day, later wrote about what happened next. He saw Philip fall "upon his face in the mud and water, with his gun under him." According to Church, when news of King Philip's death spread, "the whole army gave three loud [cheers]." Were these cheers for justice or revenge? Later events make this a hard question to answer.

Church announced that since King Philip "had caused many an Englishman's body to be unburied, and to rot above ground, not one of his bones should be buried." Church had Philip's body dragged out of the

A confrontation during King Philip's War

swamp. Church then followed English laws of that time, which permitted the bodies of murderers to be mutilated and displayed. King Philip's body was cut into four pieces and hung from four different trees. His head was cut off, too, and on August 17, it was placed on a tall pole in Plymouth, Massachusetts. It remained there for more than 20 years. Some colonists traveled many miles to see this horrible sight. King Philip's leadership had brought death and destruction to their communities.

There were no English laws, though, for what Church did with Philip's battle-scarred hand. Church gave this "paw," as he called it, to the man who had killed Philip. That man kept the hand in a pail, earning money by showing the awful souvenir to anyone who paid to see it.

Church had called Philip "a great beast." Many other colonists also considered native peoples to be less than human. A well-known minister named Increase Mather wrote that "Indians are speaking Apes." This prejudiced belief caused many hardships for the Wampanoag, both

6

before and after King Philip's War. Contact with Europeans brought enormous changes to this people and their traditional way of life.

The English settlement of North America forever changed the Wampanoag way of life.

"PEOPLE OF THE DAWN"

The Wampanoag (pronounced wam-puh-NO-ag) are a native people of the Northeast coast. They lived in what is now southeastern Massachusetts, including the islands off its coast, and eastern Rhode Island.

This woodland region was once the home of between 12,000 and 24,000 Wampanoag. They inhabited more than 40 different communities. Today, the Wampanoag live in this same area, but their numbers and territory are much smaller. There are now between 3,000 and 5,000 Wampanoag. Most live in the Massachusetts

The Gay Head Light stands atop the Aquinnah Cliffs, traditional home of the Wampanoag on the island of Martha's Vineyard.

9

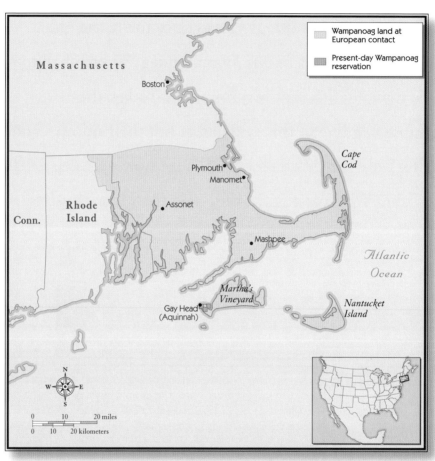

The Wampanoag live on islands and the mainland.

communities of Mashpee, Aquinnah, and Manomet. In Massachusetts, the five organized Wampanoag bands or tribes are the Assonet, Gay Head (Aquinnah), Herring Pond, Mashpee, and Namasket. The Seaconke live in Rhode Island.

10

Wampanoag saw the sun rise before those who lived farther inland. The name *Wampanoag* means "People of the Dawn" or "First Light" or "Eastern People." Like other native peoples in their area, the Wampanoag spoke an Algonquian language. Their languages were similar and easily understood by each other. Neighboring peoples included the Narragansetts, Nausetts, Nipmucks, Massachusetts, and Pequots. Sometimes the Wampanoag traded peacefully with their neighbors. Other times, they fought over territory.

The Wampanoag saw the sun rise before most other people.

FOOD AND SHELTER

The Wampanoag farmed and also hunted, fished, and gathered food. According to the seasons, they changed their homesite. Both land and sea offered food and comfort.

In the spring and summer, Wampanoag families lived in villages along the coast that were cooled by ocean breezes. Women and girls planted gardens filled with corn, beans, squash, and pumpkins. They gathered wild berries, nuts, onions, and tubers, as well as clams and other shellfish. Men fished from hardwood canoes called *mishnoonash*. They caught fish such as cod and herring and large creatures such as

A watch tower in a garden allowed the Wampanoag to scare away birds.

12

The Wampanoag lived in a round house in the warm months.

seals and whales. Men also hunted small forest animals, such as rabbits and raccoons. Some of this food was cooked and eaten right away. Stews, soups, and cornbread were popular. Some food was smoked or dried by the women, and then stored underground for later use.

In these warmer months, Wampanoag lived in round houses called *wetuash*. Their hardwood frames were covered each year with fresh reeds or bark. These lightweight materials allowed cool breezes to enter. Because the Wampanoag returned each year to the same homesite, they left wetuash frames standing.

13

In the fall and winter, Wampanoag moved inland to forests well away from bitter ocean storms. Men hunted geese, ducks, and wild turkeys. This was also the best time to hunt deer, bear, and moose. They cut holes into iced-over lakes and streams to fish. Wampanoag families also ate stored foods then. At their cold-weather homesite, the Wampanoag lived in larger, longer wetuash. Instead of just one family, up to 50 related people might live in these longhouses. Extra bark and reed mats were placed over longhouse frames to keep out icy winds and snow.

The Wampanoag lived in a longhouse in the cold months.

14

FAMILY LIFE

The land and sea provided more than food and shelter. Wampanoag men made bows, arrows, spears, and fishing weirs from wood. They sharpened animal bones and stones into arrowheads and knives. Women turned seashells as well as sticks into hoes for gardening. They wove reeds and grasses into beds. Both men and women used tough strings of deer flesh, or sinews, for tools. Men used these sinews for bowstrings, while women used them with bone or shell needles to sew clothing.

Wampanoag men and women both wore short clothes around the middle of their bodies. These breechcloths were usually

Fishing spears had carved tips.

Women wore deerskin capes.

made from deerskin. Women sometimes wore deerskin skirts, too. In summer, Wampanoag might also wear woven mantles of lightweight grass. These protected them from mosquito bites. In winter, Wampanoag added deerskin leggings and fur capes to their clothing. They wore moccasins of deerskin or, if they could get it, heavier moose skin.

Wampanoag men might wear headbands with one or two feathers. Only chiefs or other important people would sometimes wear fancier headbands with many feathers pointing straight up.

Belts were worn to hold up breechcloths and, sometimes, for decoration. Wampanoag used different patterns while stringing colorful seashells into belts called wampum. Shells and colors made patterns that told stories or identified the maker's family. Wampum makers often used purple and white quahog shells in

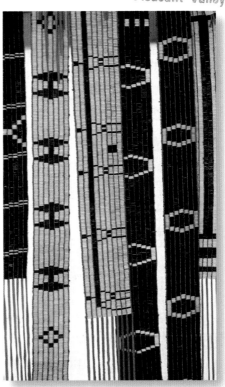

Wampum belts have interesting designs.

their creations. Besides decoration, wampum was a valued trade item. Someone who had a lot of wampum was rich.

Women made containers out of animal skin, bark, or woven grasses or reeds. They also shaped and baked pots from the colorful coastal clay. Girls and boys learned all these skills by watching and helping their parents. Young people sometimes had the job of keeping crows and other

17

pests away from the crops. Babies were kept snug and safe in wood cradleboards.

Families passed along traditions as well as skills. It was fun to tell and listen to stories around the campfire. Children heard how the giant Moshup supposedly made the coast islands as he dragged one huge foot. They learned to be welcoming and friendly to visitors. About these stories, Wampanoag today say that "Moshup was the first schoolmaster. From his home on the Cliffs he taught the people respect. … He also taught us to be charitable— for when he had great stores of fish he gave."

Fathers led families. Sons inherited hunting territory from their fathers. The Wampanoag respected women, though. A wife could leave a cruel husband. A mother's family was important in another way. Her ancestors determined the clan of her children. Clan members often helped one another.

VILLAGE AND TRIBE LEADERS

A skillful and wise person, usually a man, led each village. This person was called the sachem. Sachems listened to a council of elders before deciding matters.

A statue of Ousamequin, who was known as Massasoit to the English

19

In times of war, sachems also listened to warrior leaders called *pneisog* (pronounced pa-NEE-sog). Village sachems then carried news, gave advice, and followed the directions of their tribe's main leader. Wampanoag called this grand sachem their *massasoit*. This word means "high one" or "great leader."

Sons inherited the position of sachem from their fathers. If a sachem had no sons, a daughter would inherit this important job. Sachems made trade agreements, settled arguments between families, and greeted visitors. Other Wampanoag gave some of their food and goods as tribute to their sachems. The sachems, though, had to be responsible and smart to keep their inherited positions. If a sachem was foolish or greedy, the council would choose a better person for the job.

Sachems received food tributes from their villagers.

20

The Nauset Marsh area on Cape Cod was the site of Wampanoag villages.

The medicine man, or *paw waw*, was another important leader. Wampanoag medicine men provided advice and help based on their special knowledge of the spirit world.

Each village had its own paw waw. The tribe also had a grand paw waw who worked with its grand sachem.

21

THE SPIRIT WORLD

The Wampanoag believed that one Great Spirit had created the world. They prayed to this spirit called Kiehtan. They also believed that each living creature and part of Earth has its own spirit. Wampanoag respected these spirits. When hunting an animal, Wampanoag would thank its spirit. They thanked the spirits of the crops for a

The Wampanoag would thank the spirit of the animals they hunted with their bow and arrows.

good harvest. They also thanked the Great Spirit Kiehtan.

The Wampanoag had many thanksgiving ceremonies. In the summer, they celebrated the first crops with a Green Corn Ceremony. In the fall, they celebrated

A Wampanoag cranberry bog

later crops with a Cranberry Thanksgiving. Wampanoag feasted, danced, and prayed at these gatherings.

The paw waw made sure that these traditions were followed correctly. He also led special ceremonies at times of war. Because the Wampanoag believed evil spirits or Kiehtan's anger caused disease, the paw waw was their doctor. He held ceremonies to cure sick people. One

A paw paw conducts a Wampanoag funeral ceremony.

healing custom was a special sweat bath in the sweat lodge. The paw waw also performed marriages and helped bury people. He helped boys and girls gain knowledge of the spirit world.

Boys chosen to be warrior leaders took part in several special ceremonies. These included running a gauntlet, going without food and water, and swallowing a special drink made from herbs.

EXPLORERS AND COLONISTS

European explorers first met the Wampanoag in the 1500s.
These Portuguese and British sailors later harmed the
Wampanoag. By 1614, several Wampanoag had been
kidnapped and sold into slavery in Europe. Some died
there. A few, like Tisquantum, also called Squanto,
managed to escape.

A Wampanoag watches the arrival of British colonists.

Between 1614 and 1620, huge numbers of Wampanoag, because they had no immunity, died from the diseases European sailors had brought. Sometimes, these epidemics killed all the people in a village. When Squanto finally returned to his home village, he was horrified to discover that all his family and friends had died.

Nonetheless, the Wampanoag were not hostile when English colonists arrived in 1620. These colonists, called Pilgrims, had crossed the Atlantic Ocean from England on a ship named the *Mayflower*. In England they had not been allowed to practice the religion of their choice. They journeyed to North America to have this freedom of religion. Led by William Bradford, the colonists built their homes in the ruins of a Wampanoag village.

The Wampanoag watched the colonists. When the massasoit Ousamequin saw that they needed help, he showed them how to raise corn and find other food. This was part of traditional Wampanoag hospitality.

Tisquantum helped the two groups, which spoke

The Wampanoag and Pilgrims shared a thanksgiving feast.

different languages, understand each other. When in the
fall of 1621, the Pilgrims celebrated their good harvest
with a thanksgiving feast, the Wampanoag joined the
celebration. They brought deer and shared other
traditional Wampanoag foods that were part of their
own thanksgiving feasts.

27

*Other treaties followed Ousamequin's
agreement with the English.*

Around the time of this first Pilgrim thanksgiving, Ousamequin signed a treaty with the settlers. He agreed the Wampanoag would not fight the English. In return, colonists would help the Wampanoag in wars or disagreements with other native peoples. At the time, the Wampanoag were at war over territory with the Narragansett. This treaty and other papers called Ousamequin by the name Massasoit, which was really his title.

While Massasoit lived, the treaty was followed and peace lasted. Events during the next years, however, brought harm to the Wampanoag. More colonists arrived. These Puritans took over land the Wampanoag traditionally used. The settlers also carried diseases that became new epidemics. Between 1630 and the 1670s, many more Wampanoag died.

28

FIGHTING TO EXIST

English colonists tricked other Wampanoag sachems into signing more treaties. Sometimes, these sachems did not understand that they were giving up all rights to their land. English courts did not listen to Wampanoag or other native peoples who had arguments with colonists.

According to one account, Wampanoag leaders complained that "if 20 of their honest Indians testified that an Englishman had done them wrong, it was nothing; but if one of their worst Indians testified against any Indian or their king, when it pleased the English, it was sufficient." In 1675, these growing problems led to war.

After Massasoit died in 1671, his oldest son Wamsutta, also known as Alexander, became the grand sachem. Within the year, though, Alexander died. The Wampanoag suspected he had been poisoned at a meeting with English leaders.

Wamsutta, also known as Alexander, may have been poisoned.

Alexander's younger brother Metacom, also known as King Philip, then became the grand sachem.

Metacom united the Wampanoag, Nipmuc, Narragansett, and Pequot peoples to fight the settlers. Metacom spoke about his father's leadership. He noted, "The Wampanoag had been the first in doing good to the English and the English were the first in doing wrong." Metacom explained that the English now had "100 times more land" than the Wampanoag, but still were not satisfied. Metacom fought for his people's survival.

King Philip's War took place from 1675 to 1676. It was a time of terror and death for everyone involved. Many colonists were killed, but more native people lost their lives. English fighters killed women and children as well as warriors. A thousand or more unarmed women and children died at the Great Swamp Fight or Massacre. Most were Narragansett, but some were Wampanoag taking shelter with these allies. The colonists also burned crops.

One widely read account of this time was written by Mary Rowlandson. She had been captured by the Wampanoag

A monument near West Kingston, Rhode Island, marks the site of the Great Swamp Fight.

31

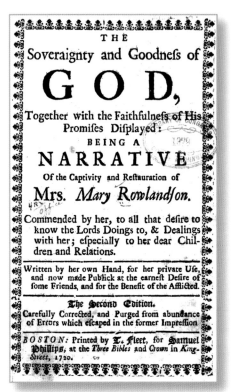

THE
Soveraignty and Goodnefs of
GOD,
Together with the Faithfulnefs of His
Promifes Difplayed:
BEING A
NARRATIVE
Of the Captivity and Reftauration of
Mrs. Mary Rowlandfon.
Commended by her, to all that defire to
know the Lords Doings to, & Dealings
with her; efpecially to her dear Chil-
dren and Relations.
Written by her own Hand, for her private Ufe,
and now made Publick at the earneft Defire of
fome Friends, and for the Benefit of the Afflicted.
The Second Edition.
Carefully Corrected, and Purged from abundance
of Errors which efcaped in the former Impreffion
BOSTON: Printed by T. Fleet, for Samuel
Phillips, at the Three Bibles and Crown in King-
Street, 1720.

*Mary Rowlandson's book was
a best-seller of its time.*

and Narragansett and held prisoner for three months. A minister's wife, she described her enemies as "roaring lions, and savage bears," yet she also wrote about acts of kindness some native people showed her. One couple, she recalled, always fed her "if I went into their wigwam at any time … and yet they were strangers that I never saw before."

The English did not show kindness when they won this war. It did not end officially on one particular day. Instead, after King Philip's death and mutilation, the Wampanoag and their allies gradually stopped fighting. The English made slaves of Philip's family and some other Wampanoag. By 1676, only about 400 Wampanoag were left to live on their traditional land.

CHANGE AND SURVIVAL

After King Philip's War, some Wampanoag continued their traditional ways. Others joined native peoples in the "praying towns" that Christian missionaries had started. Natives there were required to attend church and give up their religion and other customs. Some Wampanoag moved to special villages where colonists taught English ways of farming. Disease brought terrible changes. In

Smallpox killed many Wampanoag.

33

Sailors get ready to capture a whale.

1763, another epidemic killed most of the Wampanoag
remaining on Nantucket Island.

Some Wampanoag took jobs on whaling ships.
While most worked for little pay, one Wampanoag man
became a ship's captain. Amos Haskins commanded the

34

ship he proudly named *Massasoit*. These sailors and some other Wampanoags dressed, worked, and lived much like the settlers around them. Yet the Wampanoag did not lose their traditional values. Some kept customs alive.

Some Wampanoag continued to protest their treatment by government officials. One influential protestor was a man named Paul Cuffe. He had had a Wampanoag mother and a free African-American father. Through his own cleverness, Cuffe became a wealthy trader and ship owner. He then campaigned for the rights of native peoples and blacks. He also helped freed black slaves return to Africa.

During the Revolutionary War, 70 Wampanoag warriors fought alongside American colonists against the British. Yet the Wampanoag people did not benefit from being the colonists' allies. After the United States won independence from England in 1783, U.S. officials governed native peoples. Often, they made rules that harmed the Wampanoag living on reservations.

The Indian Meeting House in Mashpee was built in 1684. The Mashpee continue their work to be recognized as a tribe.

The state of Massachusetts also had laws that affected many Wampanoag. One 1789 regulation made it illegal to teach Wampanoag on one reservation to read and write. In 1849, Massachusetts also announced that the Wampanoag in Mashpee were no longer a tribe. This decision caused the Mashpee to lose some of their land.

The Wampanoag people did not give up. In 1928, they reorganized as the Wampanoag Nation.

"WE'RE STILL HERE"

Many native peoples' rights depend on the United States accepting their group as an official tribe. In 1978, the Mashpee failed to gain such official recognition. In 1987, though, the Gay Head (Aquinnah) tribe did win government recognition. In 1996, the Aquinnah joined with other tribes and native peoples in the Wampanoag Confederation. This organization works to defend and regain rights.

Wampanoag homelands near Plymouth

37

Chief Wilfred Greene

In 2003, the Seaconke in Rhode Island filed a court case against their state. Chief Sachem Wilfred Greene claims that 34 acres of northern Rhode Island was the historic homeland of King Philip. The Seaconke want this traditional land returned, or they want to receive money for the land. Another problem the Wampanoag face now is waste dumps that may harm their coastlands and water.

The Gay Head (Aquinnah) tribe governs itself through an elected council. The Mashpee elect leaders, too. The Wampanoag also continue to honor wise leaders who as sachems or paw waws pass along traditional knowledge. The unity circle around a clambake is one traditional way Wampanoag continue to offer praise and thanks. Yearly

The Wampanoag celebrate their traditions at festivals and powwows.

festivals such as the Legend of Moshup Pageant, held at
Gay Head, are another way the Wampanoag celebrate and
share their heritage. Participants in traditional clothing tell
their people's important stories then.

In many ways, the everyday life of Wampanoag
today is much like that of their non-Wampanoag

39

A Wampanoag woman makes traditional shell jewelry.

neighbors. They go to school, work, shop, and play like other citizens of Massachusetts and Rhode Island.

Many Wampanoag, however, want to repair damage done to their culture. In the 1990s, the Aquinnah began a project to learn and teach their traditional language, Wopanaak. They hope to make it a living language once more. Individual Wampanoag are also active in practicing and sharing their customs with others. Some work or volunteer at Plimoth Plantation and other museums.

The tribal seal

The Wampanoag people have suffered many losses, but they are determined to survive and grow. Their determination was summed up recently by the Mashpee Wampanoag man who is a member of the Commission of Indian Affairs in Massachusetts. Maurice L. Foxx, also known as Strong Bear, wants everyone to know that "native people are still here. We've changed somewhat, but we're still here."

GLOSSARY

culture—a group of people's beliefs, customs, and way of life

epidemics—terrible diseases that spread quickly and make many people in an area sick at the same time

gauntlet—a double row of people who by tradition hit or yell at the person running down the middle of the row

immunity—the ability of the body to resist a disease

massacre—the violent killing of a large group of helpless people

mutilated—hurt or damaged in terrible, frightening, or painful ways

prejudiced—hating or treating unfairly a group of people who belong to a certain race or religion

tribute—things or praise given to someone because of the person's important job or achievements

tubers—vegetables that grow underground, such as potatoes

weirs—wooden traps set to catch fish and other creatures

DID YOU KNOW?

- The first Bible printed in North America was written in a language that the Wampanoag probably spoke.

- The first Native Americans to attend Harvard University were Wampanoag. They were Caleb Cheeshahteaumuck, who graduated in 1665, and Joel Iacoomes (Hiascomes).

- The lullaby "Rock-a-Bye-Baby" may have come from a song Wampanoag sung to their babies as they hung in cradleboards from trees.

- Today, *powwow* means a traditional Native American gathering. This word comes from the Wampanoag word for healer, paw waw. In the 17th century, English people misunderstood this word and thought it meant the gatherings that paw waws led to heal people.

- *Massachusetts* means "place of the little mountain" in the Wampanoag language.

- The Gay Head community gets its name from the many bright or "gay" colors of the clay there. Wampanoag potters use this colorful clay in their work.

IMPORTANT DATES

Timeline

1500s	Wampanoag have the first contact with European explorers and traders.
1614	Squanto (Tisquantum) is kidnapped and taken to Europe; epidemics kill huge numbers of Wampanoag through 1620.
1620	Pilgrims aboard the *Mayflower* arrive in Plymouth.
1621	Massasoit (Ousamequin) signs a treaty of friendship with the Pilgrims; the first Pilgrim thanksgiving is celebrated.
1675–1676	King Philip's War is fought.
1763	Epidemic kills most of the Wampanoag in Nantucket.
1849	Massachusetts drops its official recognition of the Mashpee tribe.
1928	Wampanoag reorganize as the Wampanoag Nation.
1996	The Wampanoag Confederation is formed.

44

IMPORTANT PEOPLE

WILLIAM BRADFORD (1590–1657)

Led the Pilgrims both before and after their arrival in Massachusetts; he wrote an account of the colony's early years

PAUL CUFFE (1759–1817)

Wealthy trader and ship's captain who worked for the rights of native people and blacks; he had a Wampanoag mother and free black father

METACOM (KING PHILIP) (1640–1676)

Wampanoag paramount chief (and son of Ousamequin) who united his people with other native tribes to fight English colonists in King Philip's War; he was killed and his body mutilated

OUSAMEQUIN (MASSASOIT) (1590–1661)

The father of Metacom, he was the paramount chief of the Wampanoag when the Pilgrims arrived; he helped them and shared the first Pilgrim thanksgiving

TISQUANTUM (SQUANTO) (1590–1622)

Massachusetts native kidnapped by English sailors; after his escape and return home, he helped the Pilgrims and Ousamequin talk together

45

WANT TO KNOW MORE?

At the Library

Bial, Raymond. *The Wampanoag.* New York: Marshall Cavendish, 2004.

Manitonquat (Medicine Story). *The Children of the Morning Light: Wampanoag Tales.* New York: Macmillan, 1994.

Peters, Russell M. *Clambake: A Wampanoag Tradition.* Minneapolis: Lerner, 2003.

Sewall, Marcia. *Thunder from the Clear Sky.* New York: Atheneum, 1995.

Waters, Kate. *Tapenum's Day: A Wampanoag Indian Boy in Pilgrim Times.* New York: Scholastic, 1996.

On the Web

For more information on the *Wampanoag*, use FactHound to track down Web sites related to this book.

1. Go to *www.facthound.com*

2. Type in a search word related to this book or this book ID: 0756508479.

3. Click on the *Fetch It* button.

Your trusty FactHound will fetch the best Web sites for you!

On the Road

Plimoth Plantation

137 Warren Ave.

Plymouth, MA 02360

508/746-1622

To visit a living history museum and see how the Wampanoag and Pilgrims lived in 1627

Boston Children's Museum

300 Congress St.

Boston, MA 02210

617/426-6500

To see, walk through, and touch the "We're Still Here" exhibit about native peoples in New England

Look for more We the People books about this era:

The Alamo

The Arapaho and Their History

The Battle of the Little Bighorn

The Buffalo Soldiers

The California Gold Rush

The Chumash and Their History

The Creek and Their History

The Erie Canal

Great Women of the Old West

The Lewis and Clark Expedition

The Louisiana Purchase

The Mexican War

The Ojibwe and Their History

The Oregon Trail

The Pony Express

The Powhatan and Their History

The Santa Fe Trail

The Transcontinental Railroad

The Trail of Tears

The War of 1812

A complete list of We the People titles is available on our Web site: www.compasspointbooks.com

INDEX

About the Author

Natalie M. Rosinsky writes about history, social studies, economics, science, and other fun things. One of her two cats usually sits on her computer as she works in Mankato, Minnesota. Natalie earned graduate degrees from the University of Wisconsin and has been a high school and college teacher.